BRANCH

BRANCH

Glasses to Gases

From
Glasses
to Gases
———
*The Science
of Matter*

EXPERIMENT!

From Glasses to Gases

The Science of Matter

Dr. David Darling

DILLON PRESS
New York

Maxwell Macmillan Canada
Toronto

Maxwell Macmillan International
New York   Oxford   Singapore   Sydney

Photographic Acknowledgments

All photographs have been reproduced courtesy of Unicorn Stock Photos.

Back cover: Joan Bushno (top); Jim Hays (bottom)
Aneal Vohra, 10; Kathy Hamer, 11; Arni Katz, 12 (top); Judy Hile, 12 (bottom); Greg Greer, 17, 22; Joel Dexter, 21; A. Gurmankin, 30; Jim Hays, 36 (top); Tom McCarthy, 36 (bottom); Russell R. Grundke, 44; Betts Anderson, 51

Library of Congress Cataloging-in-Publication Data
Darling, David J.
   From glasses to gases : the science of matter / by David Darling.
      p. cm. — (Experiment!)
   Includes index.
   Summary: Text and experiments introduce matter and the various forms it can take under different conditions.
   ISBN 0-87518-500-2
   1. Matter—Juvenile literature. [1. Matter—Experiments. 2. Experiments.] I. Title. II Series: Darling, David J. Experiment!
QC173.36.D37 1992
530.4—dc20   91-38233

Copyright © 1992 by Dillon Press, Macmillan Publishing Company

Dillon Press
Macmillan Publishing Company
866 Third Avenue
New York, NY 10022

Maxwell Macmillan Canada, Inc.
1200 Eglinton Avenue East
Suite 200
Don Mills, Ontario M3C 3N1

Macmillan Publishing Company is part of the Maxwell Communication Group of Companies.

First edition

Printed in the United States of America
10 9 8 7 6 5 4 3 2 1

Contents

What is Science?

Imagine gazing to the edge of the universe with the help of a giant telescope, or designing a future car using a computer that can do over a billion calculations a second. Think what it would be like to investigate the strange calls of the humpback whale, dig up the bones of a new type of dinosaur, or drill a hole ten miles into the earth.

As you read this, men and women around the world are doing exactly these things. Others are trying to find out how the human brain works, how to build better rocket engines, and how to develop new energy sources for the twenty-first century. There are researchers working at the South Pole, in the Amazon jungle,

under the sea, in space, and in laboratories on every continent. All these people are scientists. But what does that mean? Just what is science?

Observation

Science is simply a way of looking at the world with an open, inquiring mind. It usually starts with an observation. For example, you might observe that the leaves of some trees turn brown, yellow, or red in fall. That may seem obvious. But to a scientist, it raises all sorts of interesting questions. What substances in a leaf cause the various colors? What happens when the color changes? Does the leaf swap its green-colored chemical for a brown one? Or are the chemicals that cause the fall colors there all the time but remain hidden from view when the green substance is present?

Hypothesis

At this stage, you might come up with your own explanation for what is going on inside the leaf. This early explanation—a sort of intelligent guess—is called a working hypothesis. To be useful, a hypothesis should lead to predictions that can be tested. For instance, your hypothesis might be that leaves always contain brown, yellow, or red chemicals. It is just that when the green substance is there it masks or covers over the other colors. This is a good scientific hypothesis because a test can be done that could prove it wrong.

Experiment

As a next step, you might devise an experiment to look more deeply into the problem. A well-designed experiment allows you to isolate the factors you think are important, while controlling or leaving out the rest.

Somehow you have to extract the colored chemicals from a batch of green

leaves and those from a batch of brown leaves. You might do this, for example, by crushing the leaves and putting a drop of "leaf juice" partway up a narrow strip of blotting paper. Hanging the blotting paper so that it dips in a bowl of water would then cause different colored chemicals from the leaf to be carried to different heights up the paper. By comparing the blotting paper records from the green leaves and the brown leaves, you would be able to tell which chemicals were the same and which were different. Then, depending on the results, you could conclude either that your first hypothesis seemed right or that it needed to be replaced.

Real Science

What we have just described is perhaps the "standard" or "ideal" way to do science. But just as real houses are never spotlessly clean, real science is never quite as neat and tidy as we might wish. Experiments and investigations do not always go the

way scientists expect. Being human, scientists cannot control all the parts of an experiment. Sometimes they are surprised by the results, and often important discoveries are made completely by chance.

Breakthroughs in science do not even have to begin with an observation of the outside world. Albert Einstein, for instance, used "thought experiments" as the starting point for his greatest pieces of work—the

special and general theories of relativity. One of his earliest thought experiments was to imagine what it would be like to ride on a light beam. The fact is, scientists use all sorts of different approaches, depending on the problem and the circumstances.

Some important things, however, are common to all science. First, scientists must always be ready to admit mistakes or that their knowledge is incomplete. Scientific ideas are thrown out and replaced if they no longer agree with what is ob-served. There is no final "truth" in science—only an ongoing quest for better and better explanations of the real world.

Second, all good experiments must be able to be repeated so that other scientists can check the results. It is always possible to make an error, especially in a compli-cated experiment. So, it is essential that other people, in other places, can perform the same experiment to see if they agree with the findings.

Third, to be effective, science must be shared. In other words, scientists from all over the world must exchange their ideas and results freely through journals and meetings. Not only that, but the general public must be kept informed of what scientists are doing so that they, too, can help to shape the future of scientific research.

To become a better scientist yourself is quite simple. Keep an open mind, ask lots of questions, and most important of all—experiment!

CHAPTER 1

Matter of Interest

Think about how many different materials we use in our everyday lives—wood, paper, plastic, metal, glass, cotton, rubber, stone, and dozens of others. Some of these materials are natural, the rest are human-made.

How we use a substance depends upon its properties. For instance, rubber works well for the sole of an athletic shoe because it bends and then goes back to its original shape. It also grips well and is very tough. Glass, on the other hand, would make a terrible shoe, but is ideal for use in windows.

Scientists spend a lot of time trying to develop new materials to do new jobs or to do old jobs better. This has led to such breakthroughs as nonstick frying pans,

◀▲ *Both outside (left) and inside (above) our homes we are surrounded with materials.*

toughened glass, heat-resistant tiles for the space shuttle, and even clothes that change color.

Three States of Matter

Everything around us—every material or substance—is made of matter. Matter is anything that takes up space. It can exist in three states: solid, liquid, or gas. Under normal conditions, most substances occur

in just one of these states. For example, we think of iron as being a solid. But if it is heated enough, iron will turn into a liquid, and eventually into a gas. As a substance changes its state, so do many of its properties.

All substances are made up of tiny particles called atoms. In most substances, atoms are joined together in groups known as molecules.

Molecules are always moving. In a solid, the molecules are very close together and can only vibrate in fixed positions. In a liquid, the molecules are usually a bit farther apart and can move around one another. In a gas, the molecules are far apart and are able to dart rapidly in any direction.

Little and Large
Atoms and molecules are much too small to be seen individually by the human eye. But we can certainly see the effect of trillions

◀ *Both motorcycles and icicles are made up of matter.*

Sorting Materials

You Will Need:

- **A collection of small pieces of materials of different kinds, such as wood, plastic, rubber, steel, copper, glass, stone, leather, cardboard, pencil lead (graphite),**
- **and cork**
- **A bowl of water**
- **A nail**
- **A magnet**
- **A bulb holder and light bulb**
- **Four pieces of wire**
- **A battery**
- **A block of wood**
- **Two thumbtacks**
- **Several pieces of different kinds of fabric***

Note: Items marked "*" are used only in the "Taking It Further" part of an experiment.

What to Do:

Choose one of the materials. What is its color? Is it rough, dull, or shiny? Use the nail to find out whether the material is easy or difficult to scratch. Does the material float when placed in the bowl of water? Is it attracted by the magnet?

Connect the light bulb to the bat-tery. Join two of the wires to the battery and then to the block of wood, using the thumbtacks as shown. Test to see if electricity will pass easily through the material by laying it across the thumb-tacks. The bulb will light up if electric-ity can get through.

Repeat these tests with the other materials. Make a table of your results under the headings shown. Arrange the materials in groups according to their properties. For example, you might

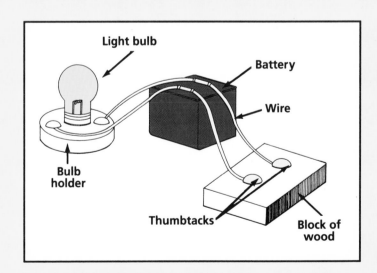

continued on next page

group the materials under the headings "Easy to Scratch" and "Hard to Scratch" and then under the headings "Will Float" and "Will Not Float." Do the materials that scratch easily also tend to be the ones that will float? If so, can you suggest an explanation? Make other such comparisons and try to explain your results.

Taking It Further:
Think about other properties that materials possess. Devise your own experiments to test these properties.

Collect several pieces of different kinds of fabric. Design an experiment to find out which of the fabrics is the hardest-wearing.

For more on this, see "Experiment in Depth," page 53, section 1.

and trillions of these tiny particles stuck together.

The properties of a substance are related to the properties of its molecules. For example, a hard-wearing material is one whose molecules are bound firmly together. A material, such as steel, that can be turned into a magnet is one whose molecules can behave like miniature magnets. A substance that is yellow contains molecules that only reflect yellow light.

Diamond: A Hard Act to Follow

Diamonds, pencil lead, and charcoal may not look much alike, but they are all made from the same kind of atoms: carbon atoms. In diamonds, the carbon atoms are linked by very strong bonds. This makes diamonds extremely hard. Another reason for their hardness is that the atoms are not arranged in layers, so they cannot slide over one another. Each carbon atom in a

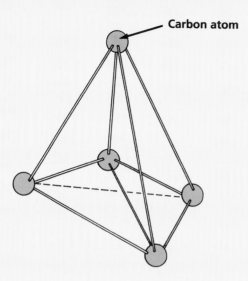

Carbon atom

diamond is at the center of a triangular pyramid, surrounded by four other atoms at the corners of the pyramid. This pattern repeats itself millions and millions of times, so a diamond is really a single giant molecule.

Diamonds are the hardest substance known. This makes them ideal for use in cutting equipment, such as glass cutters and diamond-edged saws. Powdered diamonds are also used as abrasives for smoothing very hard materials. Diamonds are found in rocks in certain parts of the earth, but they can also be made artificially in laboratories. Good, natural diamonds are extremely rare and are used mostly in jewelry.

Floating Ideas

You Will Need:

- **Small samples of different materials, including expanded polystyrene (the white, crumbly material used in packaging), cork, plastic, wood, stone, iron, and lead**
- **An apple, an orange, a beet, an onion (or any other types of fruits and vegetables that are available)**
- **A bowl of water**

What to Do:

Weigh each object in your hand. How heavy does it feel? Put it in the bowl of water. Does it float or sink? How well does it float, or how quickly does it sink? Keep a record of your results. Investigate other materials in the same way.

Styrofoam packing peanuts

Table of Densities

Material	Density (ounces/cubic inch)
Empty space	0
Polystyrene	0.1
Cork	0.2
Wood	about 0.8
Water	1.3
Stone	about 4.0
Iron	9.0
Lead	14.0
Gold	25.0

Dense, Denser, Densest

Polystyrene and cork feel light. Metals feel heavy. This is because metals are more dense.

Density is a measure of how much matter is contained within a certain volume. Water has a density of 1.3 ounces per cubic inch. Anything will float in water if its density is less than the density of water. Look at the table of densities and you will see why a cork floats and a stone sinks.

Fruits and vegetables contain mostly water, so they either sink or float. For example, apples and oranges tend to float, but carrots and tomatoes tend to sink. Oranges sometimes sink when peeled because the fruit is denser than the peel.

A substance may be dense because it contains heavy atoms, or because its atoms are packed closely together, or for both of these reasons. Are denser substances harder than less dense ones? Sometimes they are. For example, stone is harder than polystyrene. On the other hand, lead and gold are both much softer than iron, even though they have higher densities. Hardness is decided not just by how well a substance's atoms are packed together but by how strongly they are bonded.

Believe It or Not!

THE DENSEST SUBSTANCE ON EARTH IS THE POISONOUS METAL OSMIUM. A BLOCK OF OSMIUM THE SIZE OF AN AVERAGE CANDY BAR WOULD WEIGH ABOUT 2-1/2 POUNDS.

CHAPTER 2

Solids and Solutions

The next time you take a sip of cola, think about what you are drinking. It's mostly water, with some sugar, carbon dioxide gas (to make it fizz), and a few drops of flavorings and colorings. Cola is a solution—a mixture of several things that look and behave like a single thing.

A solution is made by dissolving one or more substances in a liquid such as water or alcohol. Ordinary table salt, or sodium chloride, dissolves well in water. It has a high solubility. Huge amounts of sodium chloride, together with other kinds of salts, are dissolved in the world's oceans and seas.

Solutions can also contain a mixture of liquids and gases. The water in swimming

▲ *Cola is made up of several substances that form a solution.*

pools, for example, contains a dissolved gas called chlorine. This kills germs so that the water is safe for swimming.

Solubility, like hardness and density, is an important property of matter.

Making Solutions

You Will Need:

- A measuring cup
- A glass
- A teaspoon
- A magnifying glass
- A low-power microscope
- Sugar
- Other powdered or crystalline substances, such as baking soda*
- A shallow dish*

What to Do:

Look at a few crystals of table salt under the microscope. What shape are they? Sketch some of the crystals. Do the same with a few crystals of sugar. What do you think the shape of the crystals tells you about the arrangement of atoms in these substances?

Pour a cup of cold water into the glass. Add a teaspoonful of salt to the water and stir. Watch what happens through the magnifying glass. When all the salt has dissolved, add another teaspoonful and stir. Repeat this until no more salt will dissolve. How many teaspoonfuls did you use?

Empty the glass and rinse it out.

Pour in another cup of cold water. Find out how many teaspoonfuls of sugar you can dissolve. Which has the higher solubility in cold water—salt or sugar? Repeat the experiment using hot water. Does the solubility remain the same, increase, or decrease? Invent a theory to explain your results.

Taking It Further:

Test the solubility of other substances at home or in your school laboratory. Ask permission first and remember that many chemicals are poisonous if swallowed. What happens if you pour a solution into a shallow dish and allow it to stand for several days? Can you explain what happens?

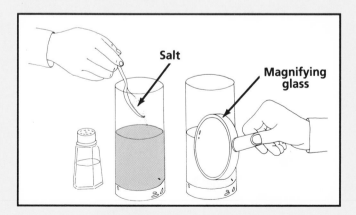

Salt

Magnifying glass

Dissolving and Melting

Sugar will dissolve and it will also melt, but the two are not the same. When sugar is dissolved in water, it makes a sweet-tasting solution. When sugar is melted in a heated pan, it turns into a brown, sticky liquid that is used in making caramel.

There are several important differences between dissolving and melting:

Dissolving

1. You start with a liquid and something else, often a solid.
2. The solid mixes into the liquid to make a new liquid.
3. You don't need heat.

Melting

1. You start with one solid only.
2. You turn that one solid into a liquid.
3. You have to heat the solid to melt it.

All substances will melt, but not all will dissolve. A substance that will not dissolve in a liquid is said to be insoluble in that liquid.

Most solids become more soluble as the temperature of the liquid increases. Gases, on the other hand, become less soluble as the temperature rises. Natural water in lakes and rivers contains dissolved gases from the air, such as oxygen and carbon dioxide. More gas dissolves if the water is colder or if the water flows over waterfalls, where it mixes more freely with air. This explains why fish caught in rivers cannot usually survive in indoor fish tanks. The water in such tanks is warmer, so it cannot dissolve enough oxygen for the fish to breathe.

Molecules That Fit Together

Molecules come in all shapes and sizes, like the pieces of jigsaw puzzles. The shape of a molecule affects how well it can work

20

The Missing Liquid

You Will Need:

- A cup of water
- A cup of rubbing alcohol
- A two-cup measuring cup

What to Do:
Pour all the water and rubbing alcohol into the measuring cup. How much liquid is in the cup? You might expect that it would be two cups, but is it? Try to explain your results.

with other molecules. Neither water nor alcohol molecules, for instance, fit together well with their own kind. But when the two liquids are combined, the alcohol molecules fit into the gaps between the water molecules. Because of this, the space the mixed molecules take up is less than the original spaces they occupied.

In Search of Solutions

A liquid that dissolves something is called a solvent. The most common, and one of the best solvents, is water. But there are many substances that will not dissolve in water. Oils and greases are insoluble in water but very soluble in other liquids, such as trichloromethane, or cleaning fluid. This

Water is a common solvent. ▶

solvent is used by dry cleaners to remove grease stains from clothes. Nail polish is insoluble in water but dissolves easily in a liquid known as acetone. Nail-polish remover is made of acetone.

▲ *Nail polish does not dissolve in water.*

CHAPTER 3

Liquids with Skins

Visit a pond in the summer and you are likely to see pond skaters dashing about over the surface. These little creatures depend for their lives on being able to stand up on and run across water. Even though the pond skater is very light, you might expect that its feet would sink into the water. But water behaves as if it has a tight elastic skin. The pond skater's legs press a little way into this skin, but don't break through. Instead the skin bends for them.

The property of liquids that makes them seem to have a skin is known as surface tension.

What Causes Surface Tension?

The molecules of a liquid are always trying to pull one another together. In the middle

How Strong Is a Liquid's Skin?

You Will Need:

- **Water**
- **Rubbing alcohol**
- **A glass**
- **A needle**
- **A paper clip**
- **A nail**
- **A small strip of paper towel**
- **A pencil**
- **Other liquids to test, such as milk***

What to Do:

Almost fill the glass with water. Make sure the needle is perfectly dry and free of grease. Use the strip of paper towel as a sling to lay the needle on the water. Do this very carefully and gently. Use the pencil to poke down the paper. Does the needle float? If not, dry it off and try a few more times. Repeat the experiment with the paper clip and the nail. Do they float or sink?

Replace the water with alcohol. Again, try to float the needle, the paper clip, and the nail. What are your results? Can you explain them?

continued on next page

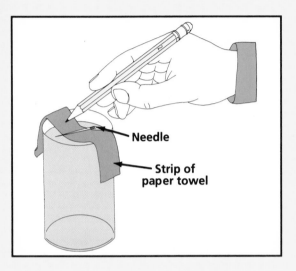

Needle

Strip of
paper towel

Taking It Further:
Repeat this experiment using other liquids, such as milk or a solution of salt or sugar in water. Which has the strongest skin?

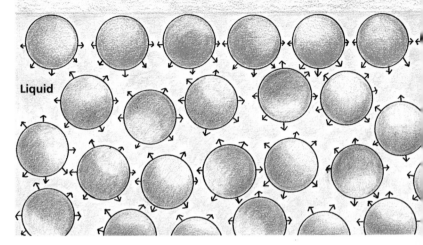

Air

Liquid

▲ *Molecules on the surface are pulled downward. But the molecules below the surface are pulled in all directions.*

of a liquid, a molecule is pulled equally hard from all directions, so the attractive forces cancel out. But a molecule on the surface is only pulled downward. This downward tug draws the surface of the liquid tightly together, so it appears to have a skin.

Water molecules attract one another quite strongly, so water has a fairly strong skin. That is, it has a high surface tension. The molecules of some other liquids, such as alcohol, pull less hard on one another, so the liquid's skin is weaker.

Water Droplets

You Will Need:

- An eyedropper
- Water
- A kitchen tile
- Wax polish
- A rag
- A magnifying glass
- Other waterproof surfaces, such as plastic, metal, waxed paper, rubber, glass, and a waterproof coat*
- Other liquids*

What to Do:
Wash the kitchen tile and dry it off thoroughly. Put some wax polish on the rag and rub the wax onto just one half of the tile. Fill the eyedropper with water. Carefully put one drop onto the unwaxed half of the tile and one drop onto the waxed half. Look at both drops from the side with the magnifying glass. Sketch what you see. Can you explain your observations?

Taking It Further:
Try putting a drop of water onto a number of other different waterproof surfaces. Only use materials that are clean and will not soak up the water. On which surfaces does the water spread out the most and on which does it form the roundest drops? Repeat the experiment using hot water and other liquids.

For more on this, see "Experiment in Depth," page 53, section 2.

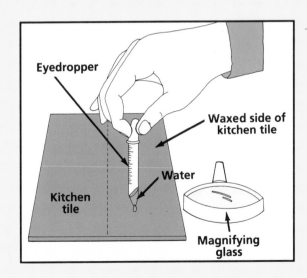

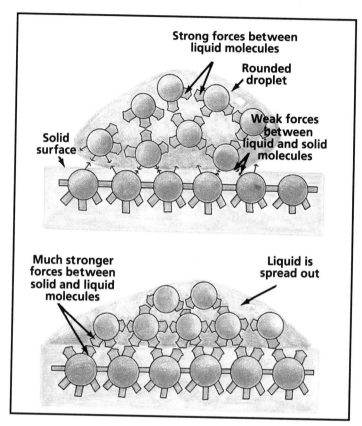

Molecular Tug-of-War

Liquid molecules are not only attracted to one another, but they may also be attracted to the molecules of solid surfaces with which they come into contact. This explains why raindrops stick to windows.

If the liquid molecules are pulled more strongly by the solid surface than they are by one another, the liquid will tend to spread out. On the other hand, if the liquid molecules are drawn more strongly to one another than to the solid surface, the liquid will gather itself into small, round droplets. Water forms droplets on wax because the pull between one water molecule and another is much greater than the pull between a water molecule and a wax molecule.

▲ *The more a liquid is spread out, the stronger the force between a solid and the liquid.*

The lower the surface tension of a liquid, the more it tends to spread out over a solid surface. Also, the surface tension of a liquid usually decreases as the temperature increases.

Breaking the Tension

You Will Need:

- An eyedropper
- A clean, dry kitchen tile
- A bar of soap
- Talcum powder
- A bowl of water
- Detergent (such as dishwashing liquid)*
- Two clean rags*
- Cooking oil*
- A stopwatch*

What to Do:

Using the eyedropper, gently squeeze a drop of water onto the kitchen tile. Look at the shape of the drop from the side. Touch the bar of soap to the water drop. What happens?

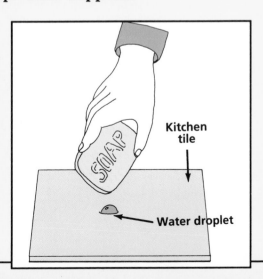

Kitchen tile

Water droplet

Partly fill the bowl with water. Lightly sprinkle the talcum powder onto the surface so that it is evenly spread. Touch the bar of soap to the middle of the bowl and watch what happens. Can you explain your observations?

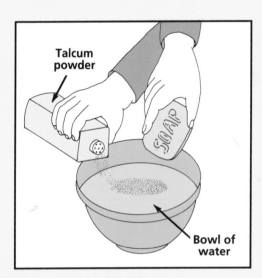

Talcum powder

Bowl of water

Taking It Further:

Empty the bowl and refill it with water. Take one of the clean rags and soil it with a few drops of cooking oil and dirt from the ground. Put the dirty rag into the bowl and swirl it around for two minutes. Spread out the rag to dry.

continued on next page

Take the other rag and rub in the same amount of oil and dirt as before. Replace the water in the bowl with fresh water and a small amount of detergent. Swirl the rag around for two minutes and then set it out to dry. When both rags are dry, compare them. Which is the cleanest? Can you explain what has happened? You might want to take this experiment even further by comparing the effects of different kinds of detergents on various types of stains. Does hot water help to clean better than cold water? If so, why?

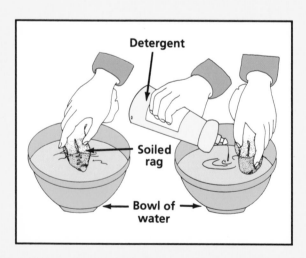

Detergent

Soiled rag

Bowl of water

Coming Clean

After a long summer day, you probably feel like taking a shower. But water on its own does not do a very good job of removing the grease and dirt that stick to your skin. To get clean, you need to rub on soap as you wash. But how does soap work?

Soap weakens the surface tension of water. This lets the water spread out and actually touch the surface it is in contact with. On its own, water would not be enough, because the natural oils on your skin, which trap dirt, will not dissolve in water. Fortunately, soap molecules have a special structure. One end of them is attracted by water, the other is repelled by it. What happens is that the water-repelled ends of soap molecules stick to your skin and to any greasy dirt that is on it. The water-attracted ends are turned toward the water. The result is that the soap molecules lift and surround the grease so that it can be easily washed away.

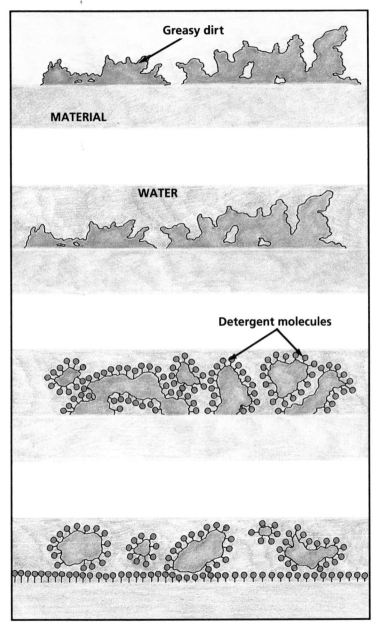

Greasy dirt

MATERIAL

WATER

Detergent molecules

▲ *Soap molecules have two "ends": one end is attracted by water and one is repelled by it.*

The detergents used for washing dishes and clothes work in the same way. They have been developed by scientists to have even better lathering and cleaning properties than ordinary soap.

Believe It or Not!

THE BIGGEST CREATURE THAT CAN WALK ON WATER IS THE SO-CALLED JESUS BASILISK LIZARD. IT MEASURES 4 INCHES FROM HEAD TO TAIL AND AVOIDS SINKING BY DASHING ACROSS PONDS ON ITS HUGE, SPLAYED FEET.

CHAPTER 4

How Slow the Flow?

Water is very different from honey, syrup, glycerine, or oil. It pours easily and is not thick and sticky like the others. The property that determines how easily a liquid pours is called viscosity. Water has a low viscosity; syrup has a high viscosity. Liquids with a high viscosity are said to be viscous.

▲ *Water has low viscosity.*

The Long Drop

You Will Need:

- A tall glass jar
- Enough of the following to fill the jar:
    water
    syrup
    olive oil
    glycerine
- A stopwatch
- A thermometer
- A pan
- A marble or ball bearing

What to Do:

Fill the jar with water. Hold the marble so that it is just touching the surface. Let go and immediately start the stopwatch. Record how long it takes for the marble to reach the bottom. Repeat this with each of the other liquids, remembering to clean the marble and jar thoroughly before each test. Draw a bar graph chart showing your results, with the bar showing the shortest time on the left and that showing the longest on the right. Which is the most viscous substance?

Warm the syrup in a pan until its temperature is about 100°F (38°C). Pour the syrup in the jar and time how long it takes the marble to reach the bottom. What can you deduce from your results?

Warning: These are messy substances. Be careful when using them and clean up properly afterward. Ask an adult to help you warm the syrup.

"Slower Than Molasses in January"

You may have been called that if you've ever dawdled too long over a job. Molasses looks like dark syrup—and it flows just about as slowly. When cold, it flows especially slowly. So "molasses in January" is a good way to let people know they should get a move on.

All liquids are more viscous when cold than when hot. This is because as a liquid heats up, its molecules move about faster, so they are able to slide past one another more easily.

Engines and Oil Cans

A car engine has many fast-moving and close-fitting metal parts. If these parts were to rub directly against one another, they would quickly overheat and wear out. This is why all engines need oil. The oil—a smooth, viscous liquid—acts as a cushion between the moving pieces of metal. It also carries heat away from especially hot parts

EXPERIMENT!

Rate of Wear

You Will Need:

- **Four flat pieces of wood**
- **An indelible marker pen**
- **An old metal tray**
- **A rag**
- **Sand**
- **Water**
- **Olive oil**

What to Do:

Using the marker pen, write your name in large letters across one of the pieces of wood. Lay the wood on the tray. Pour some water across the wood and then sprinkle some sand on top. Dip one face of another piece of wood in water and then lay this face across the first block. Rub the top piece of wood 100 times backward and forward against the bottom piece while pressing down steadily. Wipe off the bottom piece with the rag and set it aside.

Write your name, exactly as before, on another piece of wood and place it in the tray. Pour a thin layer of olive oil across the wood and then sprinkle the same amount of sand on as you used before. Apply another thin layer of olive oil to the last piece of wood. Repeat the rest of the test as before.

Compare the two pieces of wood that you had marked with your name. Which has been worn the most? Can you explain your findings?

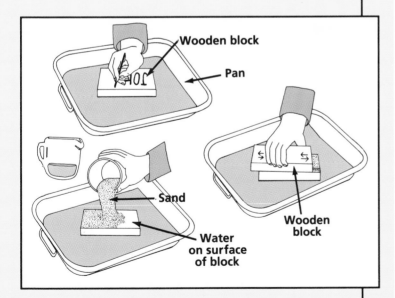

Wooden block

Pan

Sand

Water on surface of block

Wooden block

and spreads it more evenly throughout the engine.

Sticky and Springy

Some substances, including toothpaste, sit in solid lumps until they are given a push. Then they flow like a liquid. Such substances are called plastic liquids.

Toothpaste is both sticky and springy. Liquids that have these two properties are said to be viscoelastic. So toothpaste is both plastic and viscoelastic.

Most kinds of toothpaste also have tiny, hard particles inside them. These particles help scrape away the sugary layer that clings to teeth, without damaging the teeth themselves. When tiny solid particles hang in a liquid, the result is called a suspension. Toothpaste is a suspension of solids in a plastic, viscoelastic liquid.

34

Strange Paste

You Will Need:

- A tube of toothpaste
- A 6" ruler

What to Do:
Hold the tube of toothpaste upside down. Squeeze gently until the toothpaste sticks out about 1/4 inch below the nozzle. Stop squeezing. What happens?

Put a small blob of toothpaste on your finger. Tip the blob sideways, then upside down. Rub the toothpaste between your fingers. Do you think the toothpaste behaves more like a solid or a liquid?

Squeeze out two lines of toothpaste, 4 inches long and 3/4 inch apart on a smooth, clean surface. Lay the ruler along them. Push the end of the ruler gently, first along the direction of the lines and then across the lines. What happens when you let go each time? Invent a theory about how toothpaste molecules behave that would explain all your observations.

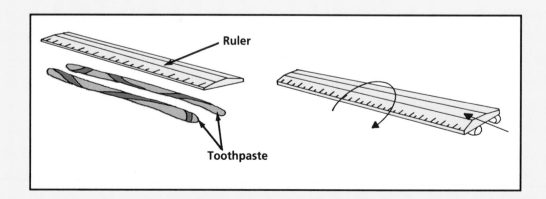

Ruler

Toothpaste

Jelly in the Can

A few years ago, special new paints, called thixotropic paints, were developed. They look like jelly in a can. You can dip a brush into them, lift the brush out, and the paint does not drip. But as soon as you move the brush against a hard surface, the paint comes off like a slippery liquid. A thixotropic liquid is like a gel until you disturb it. Then it flows freely. This kind of paint has a warning label stating "Do Not Stir," because if you stir, you break the thixotrope, and the paint runs and drips.

Ketchup is also thixotropic. That is why it often gets stuck in the bottle. By shaking the bottle you break the thixotrope and allow the sauce to run out.

CHAPTER 5

Str -e—t——c——h!

It would be a hard life without elasticity. This is the property of substances that makes them bounce back after they have been stretched out of shape. Rubber is highly elastic. That's why we use it for making tires, balls, rubber bands, the soles of shoes, and all sorts of other things that need to be springy. Metal coiled into elastic springs provides comfortable support in sofas and beds.

The springs in the car (above) are made ▲ ▶
from metal, while the joggers run on rubber
shoes. Both metal and rubber, in these
cases, are elastic.

Bouncing Back

You Will Need:

- **A table**
- **A hard floor**
- **A long strip of cardboard**
- **Sticky tape**
- **Several different kinds of small balls, for example: a tennis ball, a solid rubber ball, a "super ball" (made of compressed rubber), a Ping-Pong ball, and a golf ball**
- **A set of scales**
- **A towel**
- **An assistant**

What to Do:

Tape the strip of cardboard to the leg of the table. Hold the tennis ball over the edge of the table so that the middle of the ball is level with the tabletop. Your friend should be kneeling down, ready to see roughly how high the ball bounces. Let the ball fall. Ask your friend to hold the edge of the towel level at the height that the middle of the ball seemed to reach after its bounce. Let the ball fall again while your friend looks at eye level over the edge of the towel held at this height. If the middle of the ball reaches exactly the line of the towel after the bounce, mark this height on the cardboard and label it "tennis ball." Otherwise, drop the ball again with the towel either slightly higher or lower.

When you think you have an accurate mark for the first ball, repeat the test with the other balls. Remember to write down which ball corresponds to which line on the cardboard. Then weigh each ball on the scales. Make a chart of the height of bounce compared

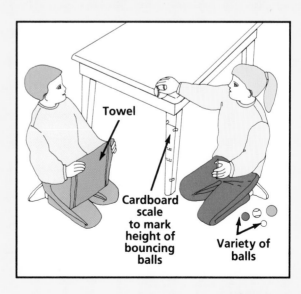

Towel

Cardboard scale to mark height of bouncing balls

Variety of balls

continued on next page

to the balls' weights. What can you conclude? Do the heaviest balls always bounce the most? Which are the best bouncers? What are they made of? Are they solid or hollow?

Taking It Further:
Put the bounciest of the balls in the freezer for one hour. Remove the ball and, to see how high it bounces, quickly carry out the above test. Has its elasticity changed? If so, is the ball more or less elastic than when it was warm?

Clues to a Disaster

After the space shuttle *Challenger* exploded a minute after takeoff in 1986, an inquiry was set up to study the disaster. The accident happened because a special seal, known as an O-ring, had failed in one of the shuttle's big solid-rocket boosters (SRBs) and allowed fuel to leak out. But why had the O-ring failed?

One of the people taking part in the inquiry was a leading American scientist, Richard Feynman. He had heard that the shuttle had taken off after a very cold night at the launch site. Icicles still hung from the spacecraft as its engines fired. During a meeting, Feynman put a piece of O-ring material into his drinking glass of ice water. A few minutes later, when he took it out, the O-ring was stiff instead of elastic. In this condition, it could no longer work as an effective seal. Through a simple experiment, Feynman had found the cause of the disaster.

Springy Molecules

The force you have to exert to pull apart a rubber band is the same as the force with which the molecules in the rubber are trying to pull one another back together again. When you stretch a rubber band, you are dragging molecules farther apart. When you relax your pulling, the molecules move back together again.

An elastic substance is one whose molecules can be separated quite a long way and still return to their original position. Rubber and skin both have this property. Other materials, like string and soft plastics, are fairly elastic. Still other materials, such as stone and glass, have a very low elasticity.

Stretching to the Limit

You Will Need:

- A long, strong rubber band
- A strip of cardboard
- A strong piece of wire, such as coat-hanger wire
- A large, strong plastic bag
- Sand
- A set of scales

What to Do:
(It would be a good idea to spread newspapers below the experiment area to avoid a mess.) Hang the rubber band from a strong nail fixed to the wall. Ask an adult for help with this. Mark a scale in tenths of an inch on the strip of cardboard. Fix the cardboard on the wall behind the band so that when the band is straightened (but not stretched) the bottom of it reaches to the zero reading. Bend the wire to make an *S*-shaped hook as shown. Weigh the hook and the plastic bag. Hang the hook from the rubber band and hang the bag from the hook.

continued on next page

Read off the new length of the band and write this down next to the weight of the hook and bag. Measure out 1 ounce of sand on the scale and pour this into the bag. Again, make a note of the rubber band's length next to the total weight hanging from it. Continue adding sand, 1 ounce at a time, recording the new length and weight. Do this until either the bag is full or the rubber band breaks. Plot a graph of the length of the band against the weight suspended from it. What shape is it? Can you explain your results?

Taking It Further:

Carry out this experiment again, but with a metal spring in place of the rubber band. What happens? Invent a theory to account for your observations.

For more on this, see "Experiment in Depth," page 55, section 3.

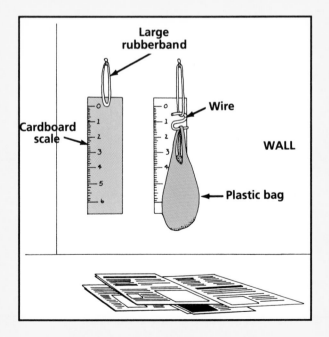

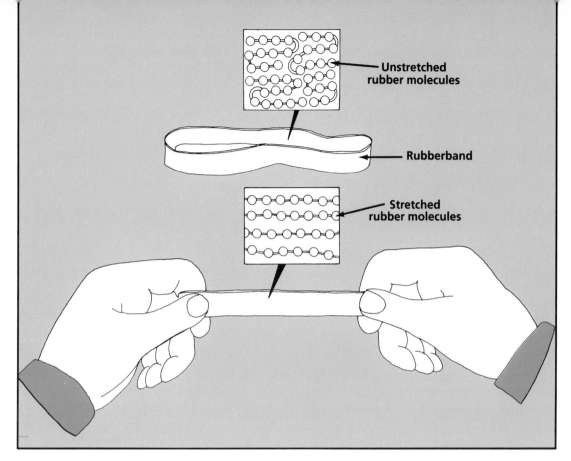

▲ *Stretched and unstretched rubber bands have different molecule structures.*

Inside Rubber

The reason why rubber can be stretched so much is that it is built up of long chains of molecules, most of which are folded like tangled ropes. When the material is pulled, the chains straighten themselves out. They return to their original tangled shape after the stretching force is removed. If the rubber molecules are pulled too hard, though, they snap apart.

Many other materials, such as wood and silk, are built of chains of molecules. But in most cases, strong links between the chains prevent them from curling back on themselves, so the material is not very elastic.

Breaking Point

You Will Need:

- **Several paper clips**
- **A stopwatch**
- **An assistant**
- **A magnifying glass***
- **A low-power microscope***
- **Different types and thicknesses of wire***

What to Do:

Straighten out all the paper clips. Hold one and bend the middle of it backward and forward as quickly as you can. Count how many times you have to bend it before it snaps. Have your assistant time how long it took from the first bend to the moment of snapping. Write down these results.

Take another paper clip and bend it backward and forward at a steady rate, but a little more slowly than the first time. Make sure you bend the clip by the same amount as the first clip and by the same amount each time. How many bends did it take to break? How long did it take?

Repeat these steps for several other clips. Each time, reduce the rate at which you bend the metal. Finally, bend a clip extremely slowly. Take several seconds over each bend. Plot your results as a graph, with the number of bends to breakage plotted on the vertical axis and the time taken per bend on the horizontal axis. What shape is your graph? What can you deduce from this?

Taking It Further:

Bend another paper clip backward and forward a few times very quickly. Put the bent part to your lip. What do you feel? Look at the bent part through the magnifying glass. Is the appearance of the metal that has been bent different from the metal in the rest of the clip? Bend the clip until it snaps. Examine one of the broken ends under the microscope. Describe your observations and make a sketch of what you see.

Carry out similar experiments with other types and thicknesses of wire. Are the results different if you bend the wire in iced water or in hot water? Try to explain your findings. Experiment with bending and breaking other types of material, such as plastic.

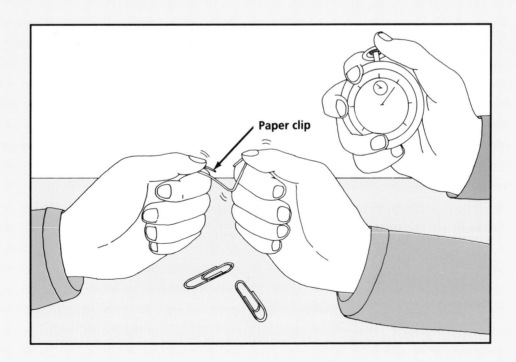

Paper clip

Metal Fatigue

Metal parts that are repeatedly put under a lot of stress may eventually lose some of their strength. This loss of strength is known as metal fatigue. It can be recognized by the appearance of tiny cracks, called fatigue cracks, on the surface of the metal.

The wings and bodies of aircraft, for example, have to be thoroughly checked at regular intervals for signs of fatigue. Engineers go over vulnerable areas with special equipment, looking for the first telltale microscopic cracks. If these cracks were to go unnoticed, they could spread throughout a vital part of the plane and cause a major failure in flight. Finding ways to avoid metal fatigue is important for anyone who builds vehicles or other machinery with hard-working metal components.

◀ *Planes are checked frequently for metal fatigue.*

CHAPTER 6

New Materials, New Properties

More new substances are being developed today than ever before. With the help of computers, scientists can now see what materials might be like even before they actually make them. They can design molecules that have specific properties. Then, they can build these molecules, atom by atom, in the laboratory.

Often, important new materials are made by putting together other substances that have useful properties. Plastics combined with nylon, for example, are stronger. A mixture of two or more materials is called a composite. One of the most widely used composites is carbon-fiber-reinforced plastic (CFRP), made by embedding tough carbon fibers in a type of plastic known as epoxy resin. Because it is strong and light, CFRP has proved to be an ideal material for high-performance sports equipment, artificial limbs, and aircraft parts.

The amazing variety of new substances currently being created and tested in laboratories around the world will have a huge effect on people's lives in the future. But not every discovery finds a practical use. Sometimes a material is found that has fantastic properties, but no one knows what to do with it.

Crazy, Mixed-Up Matter

You Will Need:

- Silly Putty
- A hammer

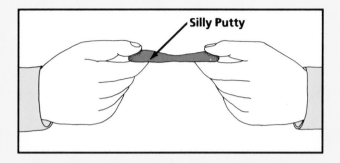

Silly Putty

What to Do:
Roll the Silly Putty into a ball and drop it on a hard floor. What happens? Com-

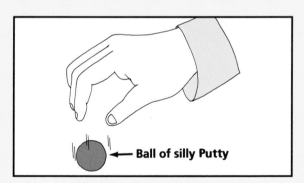

← Ball of silly Putty

pare how well it bounces with the balls you used in "Experiment! Bouncing Back," page 37. Pull the Silly Putty apart slowly. How does it behave? Pull it apart quickly. Is there any difference?

Experiment pulling the substance apart at various rates. Can you find a point at which its behavior suddenly changes? Roll the Silly Putty into a ball

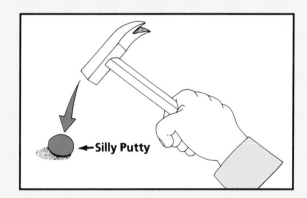

←Silly Putty

again, place it on a hard floor, and strike it sharply with a hammer. What happens?

continued on next page

Taking It Further:
Try these tests again after placing the Silly Putty in the freezer for 15 to 30 minutes. Try them again after the Silly Putty has been warmed on a radiator for a few minutes. Invent your own experiments to find out more about Silly Putty's strange properties.

For more on this, see "Experiment in Depth," page 55, section 4.

Super Ceramics
Along with new types of metals, plastics, and composites, a lot of work is being done to develop advanced ceramics. A ceramic material is basically a piece of clay that has been heated, or fired, to a high enough temperature to make it permanently hard. People have been making clay pots for over 10,000 years, and today almost every home contains a range of ceramic materials—in the form of bricks, tiles, and china plates.

The most important property of a ceramic is its ability to withstand heat. Until recently the problem has been that ceramics were very brittle. A kitchen tile, for instance, will shatter if dropped and will crack if its temperature changes too quickly. The new ceramics are harder, stronger, more heat-resistant, and better able to stand up to sudden temperature changes than ordinary clays.

Among the new materials are the aluminum-oxide ceramics used to make the insulators of engine spark plugs and the heat shields of spacecraft. These can survive temperatures of up to 3,800°F (2,073°C). In the future, ceramics will play an increasingly important part in our everyday lives.

Tomorrow's Car

Metal car engines may soon become a thing of the past. Metal is heavy and it cannot stand up to the high temperatures at which future engines will run. By the year 2000, some car engines may run three times hotter than they do today, enabling them to use less fuel and cause less pollution. Instead of steel and aluminum, their high-temperature parts will be made of advanced ceramic substances.

Other new materials will form the outer parts of future cars. The body may be made of tough composites that are as

Buried Underground

You Will Need:

- **A collection of materials, including candy wrappers, a sheet of newspaper, a paper tissue, a piece of cardboard, a plastic garbage bag, an apple core, an empty can, a plastic bottle, fast-food containers, old plastic toys, pieces of different metals, an old bicycle inner tube, and any other waste items you wish to test**
- **Sticks, for use as markers**
- **An indelible marker pen**
- **A spade**
- **A spare patch of ground**

What to Do:

Cut the materials (except those made of metal and hard plastic) into pieces of roughly the same size. Choose a patch of ground, in your yard or at school, that will not be disturbed. Ask permission first. Dig a hole 1 foot deep and place one of the materials in it. Fill in the hole and press down the soil. Push a stick in above the material and label it with the marker pen. Bury

continued on next page

and label each of the other materials in an orderly arrangement nearby. After one month dig up the materials and see whether or not they have changed. Record your observations.

Taking It Further:
This experiment could be continued over a longer period of time to study the gradual decay of the buried substances. Which materials do not seem to change at all? In what type of ground do materials decay fastest and at what time of year?

strong as steel but lighter in weight. Another possibility is the use of "smart" materials that can sense when they have been damaged and then heal themselves like human skin.

Back to Nature
Substances that break up in the ground and disappear harmlessly are called biodegradable. One big problem today is that much of the waste that we throw out in huge amounts does not decay when it is buried.

Plastic waste is especially hard to deal with. It can survive in the ground almost unaffected for many years. Because of this, researchers are now developing new types of plastics that will quickly break down. Some of these new plastics are turned to powder by exposure to sunlight. Others can be eaten by microbes in the soil.

The latest type of polyethylene carrier bag looks and feels a bit unusual. This is because it has starch molecules mixed in with the long chains of polyethylene molecules. When the bag is buried in the ground, the starch is eaten by bacteria in the soil. The rest of the plastic bag then falls apart so that little of it remains after about 18 months.

This section looks at some of the experiments described in this book in more detail.

1. Sorting Materials, page 13.
It is interesting to look at the ideas that different people come up with when asked to design an experiment. Take the case of an experiment to measure which group of fabrics is the most hard-wearing. Different pupils in a class will design different ways to carry out this test. Which is the best? Sometimes an idea for an experiment does not work well in practice because the equipment is too complicated or is simply wrong for the job. In other cases, the experiment does not isolate the topic of interest properly. If other factors are allowed to interfere with the results in an unpredictable way, the experiment is not "fair."

One method of finding how well various fabrics wear is to use a brick and a thick newspaper (to help keep the brick in place). Put the newspaper on a table and place the brick in the center of the newspaper. Hold each piece of fabric at either end and rub it backward and forward across the brick. Keep a record of how many rubs it takes to make a small hole in the material. Your test will only be fair if the rubs are equally hard and you use pieces of fabric the same size. Does a cotton sweater last longer than a woolen one? Does brand A of jeans wear better than brand B? Set goals for your experiment and present your results in a clearly written report.

2. Water Droplets, page 25.
After you have read the section "Molecular Tug-of-War" in chapter 3, you may under-

stand why water spreads out more on some surfaces than on others. Water molecules pull one another together by a force called cohesion. They may be attracted to the molecules on a solid surface by a force known as adhesion. Raindrops on a window pane stick together by cohesion and to the glass by adhesion.

What happens if the adhesive force between a liquid and a solid is very small? The liquid pulls itself into droplets. Most furniture polishes contain silicones. Silicones come in various forms—oils, greases, resins, and substitutes for rubber. They are all human-made, they all have a "backbone" of silicone atoms, and they all have the property that they will not attract water. Therefore, water on silicone wax forms into round beads and water on a silicone-coated garment runs off without wetting the fabric.

Water and glass molecules, on the other hand, stick together quite well. Pour some water into a drinking glass. Can you see how the water at the edge climbs a little way up the sides? This is because of the adhesion of the water and the glass. Try putting a thin glass tube into a container of water. What happens to the water? The effect you see is called capillary action (a thin glass tube is known as a capillary tube). Capillary action is what allows water to travel up the stems of plants. You can see it even more clearly using two small squares of glass. Put a strip of cardboard between the pieces of glass at one end to space them apart and a rubber band around them to hold them together. Wet the glass squares and then dip them into a dish of water colored with food coloring. What happens? Try to understand what you see in terms of the adhesive force between glass and water.

3. Stretching to the Limit, page 39.

If weights are put on the end of an elastic material, the material stretches steadily at first. That is, the material increases its length by equal amounts if equal weights are added. The English scientist Robert Hooke first discovered this in 1678, so it is known as Hooke's Law.

However, beyond a certain point, called the elastic limit, the material starts to behave differently. If too much weight is put on a rubber band, it reaches a stage where it cannot stretch any farther. Its molecules, instead of being tangled and loose, are pulled as tight as they will go. Any more weight causes the rubber band to snap.

A metal spring or wire, if taken past the elastic limit, does the opposite of a rubber band. It starts to stretch more for each additional weight than it did when it was obeying Hooke's Law. Beyond the elastic limit, a spring becomes stretched out of shape and will not coil up again properly even if the weight is removed. A wire, if overloaded, starts to flow almost like a liquid. It goes into a plastic state. Eventually, if enough of a load is put on it, the wire develops a narrow neck and breaks. An experiment to study elasticity in a metal wire should only be done in school with the help of a teacher.

4. Crazy, Mixed-Up Matter, page 47.

Silly Putty was discovered accidentally by scientists who were trying to develop other substances, such as silicone rubber, resins, oils, and greases. This is a good example of the fact that science rarely moves ahead in well-planned steps. Often, researchers have only a vague idea of where their research may lead. The trick is to be able to recognize when something new and potentially important turns up.

Silly Putty was certainly new—and very strange—but it has never been used for anything important. For several years after its discovery, its only practical use was as a kneading material to help strengthen hands that were crippled. Then a big rubber company began using it as the core material for its golf balls. Silly Putty rebounds higher and faster than natural rubber, so the new center allowed the balls to be driven farther.

It is as a toy, however, that Silly Putty has made its name. Its strange properties come from the fact that this freak form of silicone is really a slow-moving liquid. Its molecules simply can't flow past one another above a certain speed. If you pull or hit Silly Putty hard, the molecules simply snap apart. On the other hand, if you pull gently, the molecules easily slide over one another. In between these two extremes, Silly Putty molecules display a springiness that allows them to bounce back if they are thrown against a wall or hard floor.

GLOSSARY

atom—There are 92 different kinds of atoms in nature. All substances are made of atoms or of combinations of atoms called molecules.

density—the amount of matter, or mass, in a unit volume. Density measures how concentrated a piece of matter is.

detergent—a cleaning substance. More detergents are continually being developed to remove grease and dirt more effectively.

elasticity—a measure of the springiness of a material. A substance with high elasticity can be stretched quite far and still return to its original shape.

insoluble—A substance is insoluble if it will not dissolve in a particular liquid. A substance may be soluble in one liquid but insoluble in another.

matter—anything that takes up space. This includes all solids, liquids, and gases.

metal fatigue—the weakness that may develop in a piece of metal that undergoes repeated stretching or vibration. It begins when small cracks develop on the metal's surface.

molecule—the smallest part of a substance that still has the properties of that substance. A molecule consists of atoms joined together.

plastic liquid—a liquid that will only flow when pushed or squeezed.

solubility—a measure of how well a substance dissolves in a particular liquid. The solubility of a substance may be different in one liquid (e.g., water) than in another (e.g., alcohol).

solution—a mixture of a liquid and one or more other substances. These other substances may be solids, liquids, or gases.

solvent—the liquid in which a substance is dissolved.

state—the condition of a piece of matter—whether it is a solid, a liquid, or a gas.

surface tension—the force acting across the surface of a liquid that makes the liquid seem to have an elastic skin. It is caused by unbalanced forces between molecules at the surface.

suspension—a liquid in which tiny solid particles hang without sinking to the bottom.

thixotrope—a liquid that thickens if left undisturbed but flows easily again if shaken or stirred.

viscoelastic—a liquid that is both sticky (viscous) and springy (elastic) is viscoelastic.

viscosity—a measure of how well a liquid or a gas flows. A substance with a low viscosity flows more easily than one with a high viscosity.

viscous—A liquid or gas is called viscous if it has a high viscosity. For example, syrup and tar are viscous.

INDEX

About the Author

Dr. David Darling is the author of many science books for young readers, including the Dillon Press Discovering Our Universe, World of Computers, and Could You Ever? series. Dr. Darling, who holds degrees in physics and astronomy, has also written many articles for *Astronomy* and *Odyssey* magazines. His first science book for adult readers, *Deep Time* (1989), has been described by Arthur C. Clarke as "brilliant." He currently lives with his family in England, where he writes and lectures to students in schools.